Made in the USA
Coppell, TX
01 March 2024

29654941R00073